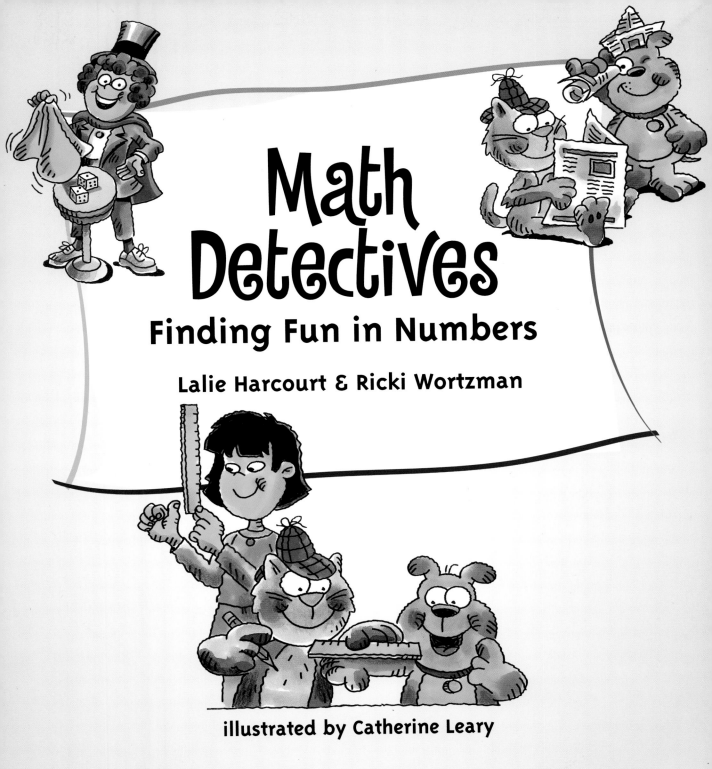

Math Detectives

Finding Fun in Numbers

Lalie Harcourt & Ricki Wortzman

illustrated by Catherine Leary

Sterling Publishing Co., Inc.
New York

For Matthew—L. H.
For Carly, Nicole, Eli, and Tess—R. W.

NOTE TO PARENTS AND TEACHERS: Some activities require the use of a pair of scissors. The activities may be done with safety scissors. Use your judgment as to whether your children will need help or supervision with these activities.

Library of Congress Cataloging-in-Publication Data

Harcourt, Lalie, 1951–

    Math detectives : finding fun in numbers / Lalie Harcourt & Ricki Wortzman ; illustrated by Catherine Leary.
      p. cm.
    Includes index.
    Summary: A collection of math games and experiments, arranged in such categories as "On the Lookout for Shapes," "Make a Tally," and "Calculator Games."
    ISBN 0-8069-7893-7 Hardcover
       1-4027-0809-2 Paperback
    1. Mathematics—Study and teaching (Elementary)—Juvenile literature. [1. Mathematical recreations.] I. Wortzman, Ricki. II. Leary, Catherine, ill. III. Title.

QA135.6 .H37 2002
372.7'044—dc21   2002021070

BOOK DESIGN BY SPINNING EGG DESIGN GROUP, INC.

10 9 8 7 6 5 4 3 2 1

First paperback edition published in 2003 by
Sterling Publishing Co., Inc.
387 Park Avenue South, New York, NY 10016
©2002 by Lalie Harcourt and Ricki Wortzman
Distributed in Canada by Sterling Publishing
c/o Canadian Manda Group, One Atlantic Avenue, Suite 105
Toronto, Ontario, Canada M6K 3E7
Distributed in Great Britain and Europe by Chris Lloyd at Orca Book Services,
Stanley House, Fleets Lane, Poole BH15 3AJ, England
Distributed in Australia by Capricorn Link (Australia) Pty. Ltd.
P.O. Box 704, Windsor, NSW 2756, Australia

Sterling ISBN 0-8069-7893-7 Hardcover

       1-4027-0809-2 Paperback

Contents

Be a Number Detective

Have you ever noticed that numbers are just about everywhere?

Once you start to look, you'll find them — many of them.

Start looking here.

There are over 20 numbers in this kitchen.

How many can you find?

How many numbers do you think you can find in your own kitchen?

Make a list.

Show the list to a friend.

Can you find more numbers together?

Write down all the numbers you find.

Keep looking and writing.

Good detectives are always on the lookout.

Cereal Count

Have you ever helped sweep the kitchen floor?

Imagine if no one ever did.

What if a baby dropped about 20 pieces of cereal in each meal? (Many do!)

Just think, 20 pieces a meal means:

60 in a day (if there are 3 meals of cereal a day)

420 in a week

21,900 in a year

How long has it been since this floor was swept?

1. Get a small bowl, a spoon, and some cereal.

2. Put about 5 spoonfuls of cereal in the bowl.

   How many pieces of cereal do you think are in your bowl?

3. Count to check. You can make piles of 10 to help you keep track.

10, 20, 30...

4. Ask someone else to estimate how many pieces are in the bowl.

   With practice, people get better at estimating.

   Detectives often need to estimate.

On the Lookout for Shapes

How good are you at finding shapes? Shapes are everywhere, just like numbers. If you start to look, you'll see them all around you.

Start in this bathroom. Bathrooms are really good places to find shapes.

Can you find all of the shapes shown here?

triangle   **square**   **rectangle**   **hexagon**   **octagon**

8

Pick another place your family uses.

It could be a playroom, a living room, or a garden, for example.

Ask people what shapes can be found there.

Then look to see how many they found.

You will discover who pays attention.

What Shape Are They?

Have you ever taken a close look at the people in your family? Now is as good a time as any. Start by looking at the people shown here. After this project, you will see how you can say that one is a square and the other two are rectangles.

What about you? Are you a square or a rectangle? It's easy to find out! Follow these steps:

1. Get scissors and a ball of string. Ask someone to help you measure your height and mark it on a piece of string. Cut the string as long as you are tall.

2. Hold an end of the string you just cut in each hand. Stretch your arms out wide, really really wide.

3. If the string stretches from hand to hand, you're a square. If there is too much string or not enough to reach, you're a rectangle. What did you find out?

Are you a family of squares? You know how to find out!

Compare Heights to Heads

How are people in your family different from one another? Probably each one is a different height. Think of ways in which they are the same. Some similarities are hard to see. To find them, you have to be a detective and investigate a bit.

If you had a string cut to your height, how many times do you think it would wrap around your head? Follow these steps and you'll find out.

1. Cut a string that is as long as you are tall. Wrap the string around your forehead.

2. Carefully remove it without unwinding. How
many times did it go around? Are you
surprised? Most people are.

What about the other people in your family?
Do you think the results will be the same for
them? You know how to find out. Go for it!

The Biggest Fist

In your family, who has the biggest fist? "Biggest" means the fist that takes up the most space. Does the tallest person have the biggest fist? Let's find out. A good place to start is with yourself.

1. Find a container that your hand can fit in. Fill it about halfway with water. Make a mark to show the water level.

2. Make a fist and put it in the water. Mark the water level on the container now.

3. Take your fist out. The amount of water that was between the marks equals the space that your hand took up.

4. Who do you think has a bigger fist than you? Who has a smaller one?

To find out, have each person put his or her fist in the water.

Mark the water level each time. The person who makes the water level rise the most has the biggest fist.

DAD
PAT
ME

Make a Tally

Have you ever stopped to think about what goes on in your house every day? Start your own investigation to find out all about the little things in life.

1. Explain to everyone in your family that you need them to help keep count of some things for a day. A tally is a good and simple way to keep count.

Here is what a tally looks like:

Each mark stands for "one."

I	One
II	Two
III	Three
IIII	Four
IIII	Five

2. Put up signs asking people to tally:

How many times does the phone ring?

HOW MANY TIMES IS THE TOILET FLUSHED?

How many phone calls are made?

How many times is the fridge door opened?

HOW MANY TIMES DOES THE DOOR BELL RING?

3. In the day you tallied, were there more telephone calls out than incoming calls?

Which rang more times, the doorbell or the phone?

How many times did the toilet get flushed?

Let people know what you found out.

Quick Reactions

Are you fast or are you slow? It probably depends. Your parents may think you're slow to clear the table or make your bed. You can prove to them that you are very fast.

You need a ruler and some time to practice. Here's what to do.

1. Hold the ruler at the top in your left hand. The highest number should be at the top.

   Hold the fingers of your right hand at the 1 inch (2.5 cm) mark.

2. Drop the ruler and catch it between the thumb and forefinger of your right hand. Try to catch the ruler at the same place you held it before (the 1 inch or 2.5 cm mark). What number did you catch the ruler on? The farther above the 1 inch mark you caught it, the farther it fell, and the longer it took to catch.

3. Repeat this a few more times. Are you getting any faster?

Show your mom or dad how fast you are.

4. How fast are they? Hold the ruler and drop it for your mom or dad to catch.

Don't let them know when you're going to drop the ruler.

Will you ever be called "slow" again?

Your ID, Please

Did you know that you can describe a person using numbers? Numbers can tell quite a bit about someone. Look at these identification (ID) cards. What do you know about the people and animals just from looking at the numbers on their cards?

DRIVER'S LICENSE
NAME: MIKE MATH
123 6th Ave.
Hexagon,
New York 10016

WEIGHT: 146 LBS.

HEIGHT: 5'4"
DATE OF BIRTH: 11/14/82   HAIR COLOR: Black
EYE COLOR: Brown
#123467089

PUBLIC LIBRARY CARD
Name: Ted D. Bear
123 Cave Blvd.
Hibernation,
Canada M4N 1G3

Card# 247356

HEALTH CARD
#3674519$\frac{1}{2}$
Name: Smarty Cat
Date of Birth: 1/15/00
Vaccination 2/30/02
Check-Up: 3/15/02
Weight: 400 g

1. Make your own ID card. All you need is a small card and a pen. Draw or paste in a picture of yourself if you want to.

2. Write down numbers that describe you.

   Here are some ideas: age ● birth date ● phone number ● address ● shoe size

3. Look at other people's ID cards. Do you see anything that you want to add to your ID card?

4. Make an ID card for your favorite doll, teddy bear, action figure, or superhero.

The Human Clock

Has someone ever told you to just wait a minute? You may have found that when you started to wait, the minute seemed way too long. Then there are times when you are told to wait a minute and the time seems way too short to be a minute. People don't think much about it when they say, "Wait a minute," do they?

You can learn to tell how long a minute is. Follow these steps and you'll become a human clock.

1. You need a digital clock, watch, stopwatch, or egg timer. Even better, use the timer on the microwave.

2. Start off by getting an idea of how long a minute feels. While looking at a watch or clock, just sit there for a whole minute and do nothing.

1, 2, 3, 4, 5, 6, 7, 8, 9, 10, 11, 12, 13, 14, 15, 16, 17, 18, 19, 20, 21, 22, 23, 24, 25, 26, 27, 28, 29, 30, 31, 32, 33, 34, 35, 36, 37, 38, 39, 40, 41, 42. . .

3. Now find out what you can do in a minute. Here are some ideas:

— How high can you count?

— How many times can you write your name?

— How many jumping jacks can you do?

— How many happy faces can you draw?

4. Now you have a good idea of how long a minute is. Next time someone says, "Wait a minute," you can use your own clock to tell them when time is up!

The Human Ruler

Have you ever needed a ruler to measure something and found that you didn't have one? Be prepared. Turn yourself into a human ruler. To get started, you'll need a regular ruler, but after that you won't need it as often. You'll just use your body.

1. Use a ruler to find something on your body that's close to an inch long (2.5 cm).

Most children find that their thumbs are about 1 inch long from the knuckle to the end. Is yours?

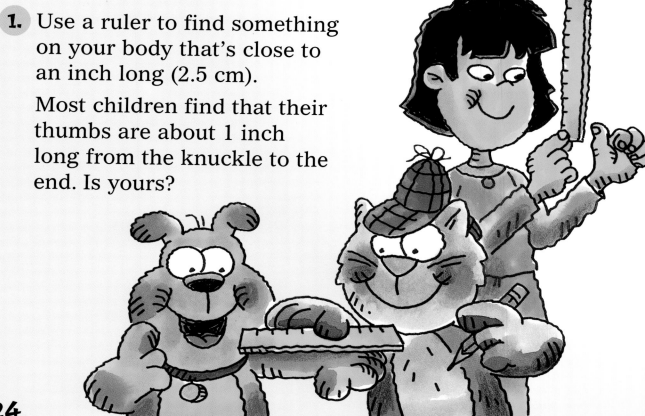

2. Find some part of your body that is about one foot long (12 inches). If you use metric units, it is 30 cm. Perhaps the distance from the tips of your fingers to your inner elbow is about one foot.

How long is your foot? What can you measure with your foot? Measure the length of your living room. Is it longer than your kitchen?

3. Use your measured body parts to measure some other things.

How many thumbs long is your notebook? How many fingers-to-elbows long is your table?

How many feet long is your bed?

Find That Card

Do you ever have to clean up around the house? Usually that means you are supposed to put things away where they belong. Maybe you have to put your clothes in the closet and your books on the shelf. Here is a card trick that you can try on people, and it all has to do with something being in the wrong place.

1. Take one deck of cards. Separate all the red cards (hearts and diamonds suits) into one pile and the black cards (clubs and spades) into another pile. Turn the piles face down. Don't let anyone else see you do this.

2. Have someone take a card from one pile, look at it, and put it in the other pile.

3. Pick up the pile into which the card was added. Look at all the cards. Keep the faces of the cards hidden from the other player. You'll have no trouble spotting the moved card. It is a different color than all the rest in the pile.

4. Hand the different card to the player and watch the look on his face!

It will drive people crazy that you can spot their cards so easily. Just tell them that things aren't where they belong!

Lucky Coins

Have you ever had a lucky coin? Do you want another one? Look through the spare change that seems to be in all homes. Where does your family keep those extra coins?

1. To find your lucky coin, write the year you were born on a slip of paper.

   Look through the coins for one with your birth year on it. The date tells the year the coin was minted.

2. Don't give up if you can't find a lucky coin. Ask people if you can look at the coins in their pockets. (You'll get to see how much change people carry around with them.)

3. Find lucky coins for people in your family and for your friends. You will need to know the year in which each person was born. Make a list of each person's name and birth year. Who was born the longest time ago?

4. Wrap the lucky coins in pretty paper and then surprise people with lucky coin gifts for no reason.

How Many?

Do you like to surprise people? Using a full glass of water and some coins, you can surprise someone. Like any good detective, you'll want to be prepared, so try this out on yourself first.

Here's the question: How many coins do you think you can put into a full glass of water? (Do steps 1 and 2 by yourself first.)

1. Get a plastic glass. Fill it to the very top with water. Get a handful of small coins.

2. Slide a coin into the glass. Just slide it very gently over the edge. Keep sliding more coins into the glass. How many did you slide in before the water overflowed?

3. Give each person a glass of water and some coins. Let each one estimate how many coins she can put in a full glass of water before actually trying to add them. Are people surprised with the results?

Walk through it

Have you ever heard the expression, "I'll believe it when I see it"? Bet that's what you'll hear if you tell people that they can walk through a piece of paper! Before you show someone else, you probably need to do the experiment for yourself.

1. Take a rectangle of paper $8\frac{1}{2} \times 7$ inches (21.5 × 18 cm).

2. Fold the paper in half so the short ends meet.

3. Mark lines almost across the paper with a pencil. You need an odd number of lines, about 13 or 15 lines. The first and last lines must start from the fold side. Never mark to the end of the line; stop about 1/2 inch (1 cm) before that (see diagram). After marking, cut through both layers of paper on the lines.

4. Now gently unfold the paper. It looks like this.

5. Cut on the center folds (red lines), but not on the folds at the edges of the paper.

6. Here's the finished paper. Are you ready to walk on through?

Don't cut ends

Double the Folds

Can you find a sheet of newspaper lying around your house? Sure you can. Now lay it flat and look at it closely. Do you think you can fold it in half 10 times? It sounds easy, doesn't it? Well, give it a try before you start betting your allowance on it.

1. Fold the sheet of newspaper in half.

2. Fold it in half again. That's two times.

3. Keep folding it in half. Remember to count each time you make a fold.

How many times were you able to fold the paper?

Do your parents think they can fold the newspaper ten times?

You might want to start by betting them that they can't do it.

How about betting double your allowance?

Games with Dice

Transparent Die

Have you ever noticed the arrangement of numbers on a die? Go get one.

1. Put your finger on the single dot. How many dots are on the opposite side of the die? Total the dots on the two opposite sides (1 + 6 = 7).

2. Now put your finger on the side with 2 dots. How many dots are on the side opposite the 2 dots?

3. Now — you guessed it — put your finger on the side with 3 dots. How many dots are on the opposite side? Total the 3 dots and the opposite number. What do you get?

4. Find someone who wants to play dice games. Before you start, tell the person that you can see through a die. Now that you know the trick, you can look at one side and tell what is on the opposite side.

The Greatest Number

1. Each player draws three lines like this: — — —
   One player rolls a die for three turns. This is one round.

2. Each time the die is rolled, both players write the number rolled on one of their lines, in whichever place they want to (ones, tens, or hundreds). At the end of the round, the player with the greatest number scores 1 point.

   <u>5</u> <u>3</u> <u>6</u>   <u>5</u> <u>6</u> <u>3</u>

3. Play another round but have the second player roll three times. Who has the largest number this time? That person gets 1 point.

4. Keep taking turns rolling the die until someone gets 5 points. That person is the winner.

Calculator Games

Do you have a calculator in your home? You probably don't use it very much. But if you knew some games to play on it, you'd use it, right? It's a good idea to learn how to use a calculator anyway! Here are some games for 2 players.

Get to 20:

1. Clear the calculator so it says 0.

2. Take turns. Each player adds 1 or 2.

3. The player who reaches 20 on his turn wins.

Back from 25

1. Start with the number 25 in the calculator display.

2. Take turns. Each player subtracts 1, 2, or 3.

3. The player who reaches 0 on her turn wins.

To 100!

1. Clear the calculator so it says 0.

2. Take turns. Each player adds any number from 1 to 9.

3. The player who reaches 100 on his turn wins.

Go ahead, get that calculator and teach someone a game. You might even make up your own.

Remember: When you play often, you may discover a winning strategy!

(Hint: Try writing down the numbers you used for a few games to see if there is a pattern.)

Imagine It

A good detective can figure out quite a bit from just one clue. Often just seeing a little tells a lot. Are you a good detective? Can you look at just a little of something and imagine more?

> YOU JUST MIGHT WANT TO SLEEP INSIDE TONIGHT.

1. Fold a piece of paper in half.

2. Cut a small shape out of the folded side.

3. Imagine what the cut-out shape will look like when you open the paper. On another paper, draw what you think you will see. Then open the cut paper and check. Is it close to what you imagined?

4. Refold the paper and try cutting out some more shapes.

5. Now try folding a new paper in half and then in half again. Cut a shape out of one folded side. Draw what you think you will see, and then open the paper to check.

6. Keep folding, cutting, drawing, and checking. With practice, you'll get good at imagining shapes.

Find some friends and show them how to play the game.

The Game of Nim

Do you like to play games? You can play nim in any room in your house. Find 15 small things — for example, buttons. Then find someone who wants to play with you and you're all set. The goal is to have the other person take the last button.

1. Put out 15 buttons or any other small objects you have around.

2. On the player's turn, he or she can take 1 or 2 buttons away. Take turns doing this.

3. The loser is the player who takes the last button.

   Teach the game of nim to a friend.

   Play often and you will be unbeatable.

About the Math You Found

Here is a little more information about some of the experiments you did and games you played.

Be a Number Detective: pages 4—5

Numbers tell us information. Numbers on clocks tell us what time it is, numbers on an oven thermometer tell the temperature inside, and numbers you see on a box of cereal tell you how much the box of cereal weighs. What is the greatest number you found in your kitchen?

Cereal Count: pages 6—7

When little amounts add up, it doesn't take long before you are dealing with big numbers. For example, look at how thick a newspaper is. Imagine a stack of 7 newspapers. Then think of how tall the stack would be for one month's worth of newspapers. When you think of all the people on the street and all the newspapers that are picked up in one month, the amount gets very large quickly.

On the Lookout for Shapes: pages 8—9

Look around your home for other tiled floors and walls. Which shapes are used to tile floors and walls? Some shapes like circles, ovals, and octagons leave spaces when you try to use them for tiling.

What Shape Are They? pages 10—11

The more that you estimate and measure, the better you get at it. Note: Even though we say "square" and "rectangle," you should know that a square is a special kind of rectangle, all of whose sides are equal in length.

Compare Heights to Heads: pages 12—13

Most people are not very good at comparing the length of straight lines to circles and curves. Mathematicians call a comparison of two quantities a ratio. The ratio of your height to the distance around your head is probably about 1 to 3, which also may be written 1:3.

The Biggest Fist: pages 14—15

When you put your fist into water, the amount of water that is moved away is equal to the amount of space your hand takes up. In fact, you are measuring the volume of your fist. Archimedes discovered this way of measuring volume. The story is that he ran down the street naked, shouting "Eureka!" after noticing that the water rose when he entered the bathtub.

Make a Tally: pages 16—17

Pieces of information that are collected are often called data. Collecting and looking at data is what statistics is about. People use statistics to help them study large quantities of data and make decisions. From the data you collected, your family might notice that people are wasting a lot of energy by opening and closing the refrigerator frequently. You might work out a plan to save electricity.

Quick Reactions: pages 18—19

You probably found out that when you dropped the ruler for yourself, the amount of time it took to catch it was much shorter than the time it took to catch it when you dropped it for another person. If the other person dropped the ruler for himself, his reaction time would be better, too. If you drop the ruler as well as catch it, you are able to anticipate or expect when the ruler is dropping. Great athletes have good reaction times, but they also know what to expect.

Your ID, Please: pages 20—21

As you get older, you will have more and more identification numbers that tell about who you are and what you do. In most countries, you will need some form of work identity number when you start to work. (You may even have one now.) This helps the government collect taxes on the amount of money you earn. You may have a library card number and a telephone number.

The Human Clock: pages 22—23

Here is how the units of time are related to each other:
1 minute = 60 seconds; 1 hour = 60 minutes; 1 day = 24 hours.

The Human Ruler: pages 24—25

There are two main systems of measurement used in the world. The customary system is probably the one that is most familiar to you if you live in the United States. In most other countries, the metric system is used. The units of measure for length in the customary system are inches, feet, yards, and miles. The units of measure for length in the metric system are centimeters, decimeters, meters, and kilometers.

Find That Card: pages 26—27

Many problems, even really big ones, are solved when people think about what doesn't belong in a situation. Many problems are solved when people think about how things are the same and how they are different. The card trick is just a simple example to start you thinking about whether things belong together.

Lucky Coins: pages 28—29

In most countries around the world, people use some sort of money. The money usually includes bills and coins. You can find the value of the bill or coin written somewhere on each one. Long ago, before people thought of using money, they would simply trade something that they had for something that they needed or wanted. If you needed something and didn't have anything the other person wanted, life was a bit difficult, so people started to use tokens. Tokens were the first forms of money. Native Americans used beads called wampum as tokens. Whales' teeth were used in Fiji.

How Many? pages 30—31

Well, you have found out that "full" isn't exactly what it seems. The water rises each time you add a coin, but it doesn't overflow for a while. That's because the tiny particles (molecules) of water on the surface have no water above them and they are pulled downward by the molecules under them. At one point there is too much water rising above the glass, and it overflows.

Walk through It: pages 32—33

The way that you cut the paper allowed the paper to stretch out. Try this activity again with an even larger sheet of paper. Can you get your a few people to hug inside the circle?

Double the Folds: pages 34—35

When you fold the paper in half, you double the number of layers. You are actually multiplying by two. When you notice how many layers are created with each fold, you'll quickly see why you can't fold the sheet ten times. Here is what happens as you keep folding:

The first fold makes 2 layers. The second fold makes 4 layers.

The third fold makes 8 layers. The fourth fold makes 16 layers....

The ninth fold makes 512 layers. By the tenth fold, the paper would be 1,024 layers thick!

Games with Dice: pages 36—37

All games that use dice have to do with chance. You're never sure how the dice will land. All you know is that one of the numbers from 1 to 6 will appear on top. The study of chance is called probability. In the case of dice, each number is equally likely to turn up on a roll. This may be hard to believe if you haven't had a lot of experience rolling dice.

Calculator Games: pages 38—39

You can play the games on pages 38 to 39 without a calculator, but it is a good idea to get used to using a calculator. Some adults think that children should not use calculators until they get really fast and accurate at adding, subtracting, dividing, and multiplying. Other adults think that using the calculator is great idea because it is the best tool for the job and it is more accurate. Find out what the adults around you think about children using calculators to do their math.

Imagine It: pages 40—41

If you fold the paper once and cut out a shape on the fold, when you open the paper you will find one symmetrical shape. The fold line is called the line of symmetry. Many objects in nature are symmetrical. Take a look at leaves, flower petals, and snowflakes. Try to find their lines of symmetry. Take a close look in the mirror. Are you symmetrical?

The Game of Nim: page 42

Nim is a game that people play all over the world. There are many different versions of the game. The one in this book starts with 15 objects. You can develop a winning strategy, which means you can win every time if you know the strategy and the other player doesn't. Just make sure that on your turn you leave 13, 10, 7, 4, or 1 object. If the other player knows the strategy too, then the player who goes first wins, because that player is able to leave 13 objects. As soon as you know the winning strategy, you can change the game by playing with a different number of objects or taking away different amounts.

Index